For

D1316861

THE CONSOLIDATED **WAGSTER'S** UNEXPURGATED **DICTIONARY** *OF HUMOR AND WIT*

Edited by
H. Gordon Havens

Design by
Scharr Design

PETER PAUPER PRESS, INC.
WHITE PLAINS · NEW YORK

INTRODUCTION

Every man has, some time in his life,
an ambition to be a wag.
SAMUEL JOHNSON

After years of extensive research, compilation,
arrangement, and editing, I am proud to present
The Consolidated Wagster's Unexpurgated
Dictionary of Humor and Wit, the punabridged
and unabashed lexicon from the best authors
spanning hundreds of years of world literature.

Any dictionary worth its salty language would
normally present the sublimity of syntax and the
exhilaration of the double pluperfect morpho-
logical infinitive. But worry about moods makes
me tense, and worry about tenses makes me
moody, so I opted to spare readers such
esoterics, and simply include 600 or so of the
most devilish definitions that any wagster could
imagine.

If readers can verify attribution of any definition
in this dictionary (and provide proof), or would
like to suggest definitions for the next edition of
The Wagster's Dictionary (tentatively entitled
Wagster's Last Tail), they are invited to submit
their contributions to this editor in care of the
publisher. My thanks in advance for your
interest and consideration.

H. Gordon Havens
Editor/Lexicographer

•••••••••

Wag•ster, *(n.)*, [ME. *waggen;* prob. shortened Fr. obs. *waghalter,* a rogue], one full of sport and fun; a comical or humorous person; joker; wit.

•••••••••

Ab·sti·nence, (*n.*), a good thing if practiced in moderation.

A·bun·dance, (*n.*), a social event in a bakery.

A·but, (*v.*), "the highpoint for a leg man."
— H.G.H.

A·cous·tic, (*adj.*), an instrument used in shooting pool.

Act of love, (*n.*), "The enjoyment is quite temporary; the cost is quite exorbitant; the position is simply ridiculous."—PHILIP DORMER STANHOPE.

Ac·tor, (*n.*), *1.* a man who tries to be everything but himself. *2.* a thespian who would prefer a small role to a long loaf. *3.* one who strives all his life to become well-known, then wears dark glasses to avoid being recognized.

Ac·tress, (*n.*), one who plays when she works and works when she plays.

Ad·dict, (*n.*), one who's completely gone to pot.

A·do, (*n.*), "what the bride and groom say to start the fuss."—ANON.

Ad·o·les·cence, (*n.*), *1.* when children ask all the questions, as distinguished from teenage, when they know all the answers. *2.* the age between puberty and adultery. *3*. when a girl stops thinking about jacks and starts wondering about Tom, Dick and Harry, *4*. the age when a girl's voice changes from no to yes. *5*. that period when children feel their parents should be told the facts of life.

A·dult, (*n*.), a person who has stopped growing at both ends and started growing in the middle.

A·dult west·ern, (*n*.), "one in which the hero still loves his horse, only now he's worried about it."—HENNY YOUNGMAN.

A·dul·te·ry, (*n*.), *1*. when a spouse is too good to be true. *2*. courting disaster.

Ad·vanced ed·u·ca·tion, (*n*.), killing yourself by degrees.

Ad·ver·tis·ing, (*n*.), the art of convincing people they've always needed something they've never heard of before.

Ad·vice, (*n*.), the only thing more blessed to give than receive.

Af·ter·math, (*n*.), the period following algebra.

Age, (*n*.), what really turns a girl into a woman.

Age of met·al, (*n*.), silver in the hair, gold in the teeth, iron in the veins, and lead in the pants.

Ag·o·ny, (*n*.), lockjaw with seasickness.

Air line food, (*n.*), *1.* pie in the sky. *2.* a contradiction in terms.

A larm, (*n.*), a device to warn burglars of police.

Al ca traz, (*n.*), the walled-off Astoria.

Al i mo ny, (*n.*), *1.* "the wages of sin."—CAROLYN WELLS. *2.* the high cost of loving. *3.* the high cost of leaving. *4.* a man's cash surrender value. *5.* the fee a woman charges for name-dropping.

Am a teur ac tor, (*n.*), a hamateur.

Am a teur o per a, (*n.*), crime on the high C's.

Am ne sia, (*n.*), loss of memory caused by borrowing money.

A nat o my les son, (*n.*), an organ recital.

Ant, (*n.*), a hard-working insect that always finds time to go on picnics.

An tique, (*n.*), *1.* an object that has made a round trip to the attic. *2.* a thing so old that it's worth more than it really is.

An tique shop, (*n.*), a junk store that has raised its prices.

A pril 15, (*n.*), when you realize that you owe most of your success to Uncle Sam.

Ar ti fi cial, (*adj.*), the judge at an art show.

Ba•by sit•ter, (*n.*), *1.* a girl you hire to watch your television. *2.* someone who takes hush money.

Bach•e•lor, (*n.*), *1.* footloose and fiancée-free. *2.* one with no children to speak of. *3.* an advocate of life, liberty and the happiness of pursuit. *4.* a man with singleness of purpose.

Back•bit•er, (*n.*), a mosquito.

Bac•te•ri•a, (*n.*), the rear of a cafeteria.

Bald man, (*n.*), one who has less hair to comb but more face to wash.

Ba•nan•a peel, (*n.*) a slipping beauty.

Band•aid, (*n.*), a fund for needy musicians.

Bank•rupt•cy, (*n.*), when your outgo exceeds your income and your upkeep is your downfall.

Bar•ber, (*n.*), *1.* a brilliant conversationalist who occasionally cuts hair. *2.* the town cutup.

Ba•roque, (*adj.*) "what a poor artist is."—H.G.H.

Base•ball sta•di•um, (*n.*), a cool place because of all the fans.

Beet, *(n.)*, a potato with high blood pressure.

Be·gin·ning, *(n.)*, the inning that decides many a ballgame.

Bet·ter off, *(adj.)*, how you feel after horseback riding.

Big·a·my, *(n.)*, *1.* when a man marries a beautiful girl and a good housewife. *2.* a crime whose punishment is two mothers-in-law. *3.* trying to have your Kate and Edith too.

Big gun, *(n.)*, frequently an individual of small caliber and immense bore.

Big wheel, *(n.)*, one who often turns out to be only a spokesman.

Big·ot, *(n.)*, a person with an exceptionally large mouth for such a small mind.

Bi·ki·ni, *(n.)*, *1.* a baiting suit. *2.* undressed to kill.

Birth con·trol, *(n.)*, no kidding.

Birth·day, *(n.)*, when a man takes a day off and a woman takes a year off.

Bleach·ers, *(n. pl.)*, blondes.

Blis·ters, *(n. pl.)*, what make cowboys sit tall in the saddle.

Blood test, *(n.)*, the final exam in vampire school.

Book keep er, (*n.*), someone whose library books are overdue.

Book worm, (*n.*), *1.* a person who would rather *read* than eat. *2.* a worm that would rather *eat* than read.

Boss, (*n.*), *1.* the fellow you can't help liking, because if you don't he'll fire you. *2.* the person who is early when you're late and late when you're early.

Bread, (*n.*), raw toast.

Breed ing, (*n.*), how one behaves in a quarrel.

Bridge, (*n.*), next to love, the greatest indoor sport in America.

Brief, (*n.*), for lawyers, a contradiction in terms.

Bron co bust er, (*n.*), a cowboy who works on and off.

Bud get, (*n.*), *1.* an orderly system of living beyond your means. *2.* an attempt to live below your yearnings.

Bur gla ry, (*n.*) the only profession that still makes housecalls.

Butch er, (*n.*) the person least likely to put on extra weight.

Butch er shop, (*n.*), where it costs an arm and a leg to buy some wings and thighs.

Cab·i·net·mak·er, (*n.*), the President.

Cam·el, (*n.*), a horse designed by a committee.

Can·di·date, (*n.*) one who stands for what he thinks the public will fall for.

Can·dle mak·er, (*n.*), a profession that only works on wickends.

Can·o·pies, (*n. pl.*), "what takes forever to eat with a knife."—H.G.H.

Ca·price, (*n.*), "The only difference between a caprice and a lifelong passion is that the caprice lasts a little longer."—OSCAR WILDE.

Ca·reer wom·an, (*n.*), *1.* one who gets out and earns a man's salary instead of staying home and taking it away from him. *2.* a female more interested in plots and plans than pots and pans.

Care·ful·ly, (*adv.*), how porcupines make love.

Cas·se·role, (*n.*), an ingenious method to get rid of leftover leftovers.

Cat, (*n.*), an animal that never cries over spilled milk.

Cel·i·ba·cy, (*n.*), too true to be good.

Charm, (*n.*), the ability to make someone think that both of you are quite wonderful.

Chaste, (*adj.*), what girls won't get if they are.

Chas·ti·ty, (*n.*), "of all sexual aberrations, perhaps the most peculiar."—REMY DE GOURMONT.

Chas·ti·ty belt, (*n.*), an anti-trust suit.

Check·mate, (*n.*), the spouse you marry for money.

Chim·ney sweep, (*n.*), one who does his work to soot himself.

Church, (*n.*), a building of prayer-conditioned comfort.

Cir·cu·lar saw, (*n.*), a rose is a rose is a rose.

Cit·y life, (*n.*), "millions of people being lonesome together."—HENRY DAVID THOREAU.

Class re·un·ion, (*n.*), a gathering where you conclude that most people your own age are a lot older than you are.

Clique, (*n.*), the sound of a French camera.

Co·co·nut, (*n.*), one who's sweet on chocolate.

Code, (*n.*), what stops up your nose.

Col·lege pro·fes·sor, (*n.*), the person who gets what's left after the athletic directors and coaches are paid off.

Com·mon law mar·riage, (*n.*), holy bedlock.

Com·pul·sive gam·bling, (*n.*), You bet your life.

Con·fi·dence, (*n.*), *1.* that feeling you have before you completely understand the situation. *2.* doing crossword puzzles with an ink pen.

Con·su·mer, (*n.*), one who is hit by everything but falling prices.

Cook, (*n.*), someone who is at home on the range.

Cook·book, (*n.*), the book with the most stirring chapters.

Co-re·spon·dent, (*n.*) the right man in the wrong place.

Cos·met·ics, (*n.pl.*), preparations used by young girls to make themselves older sooner and by their mothers to look younger longer.

Cou·ra·geous, (*adj.*), the first to use the guest towel.

Crab grass, (*n.*), "the lawn ranger."—H.G.H.

Creek, (*n.*), a river with low blood pressure.

Cri·tic, (*n.*), *1.* one who likes to hiss and tell. *2.* a mirror.

Crow, (*n.*), a bird that never complains without caws.

Dam·na·tion, (n.), Holland.

Danc·ing, (n.), the art of pulling your feet away faster than your partner can step on them.

Death, (n.), nature's way of telling us to slow down.

De·bate, (n.), what lures de fish.

Deb u·tante, (n.), a young girl with bride ideas.

Deep think·ing, (n.) thought often resulting from getting yourself in a hole.

Def·i·cit spend·ing, (n.), when you're at work making ten dollars an hour while the plumber is at your house making fifty dollars an hour.

Den, (n.), a wreckreation room.

De·nounce, (v.), what precedes de verbs.

Den·tist, (n.), someone who bores you to tears.

De·sert, (n.), long time no sea.

Di·et, (n.), a triumph of mind over platter.

Dime, (n.), what the car in front of you can stop on.

Di·men·sion, (*n.*), There are four dimensions: length, width, height and cost.

Dis·ar·ma·ment, (*n.*), Like a party, nobody wants to arrive until everyone else is there.

Di·vorce, (*n.*), proof that united we stand but divided we can stand it better.

Diz·zi·ness, (*n.*), a common malady caused by revolving credit, spiraling prices and soaring taxes.

Dog·house, (*n.*), a mutt hut.

Draft board, (*n.*), where young men are weighed and found wanted.

Dra·ma crit·ic, (*n.*), one who gives the theater the best jeers of his life.

Dream house, (*n.*), one that costs twice as much as you ever dreamed it would.

Drill ser·geant, (*n.*), a military dentist.

Drip, (*n.*), someone you can always hear but seldom turn off.

Driv·ing, (*n.*), The difference between learning to drive a car, and learning to play golf, is that in golf you don't hit anything.

Drunk driv·ing, (*n.*), putting the quart before the hearse.

Duf·fer, (*n.*), a golfer so incompetent he can even lose his ball in the washer.

Ear•ly ris•er, (*n.*), a triumph of mind over mattress.

Earth, (*n.*), a minor planet with major problems.

Eas•y as pie, (*adj.*), a piece of cake.

Ech•o, (*n.*), the only thing that can cheat some people out of the last word.

E•co•nom•ic fore•cast•er, (*n.*), a guy who tells you today what is going to happen tomorrow and explains the next day why it didn't.

E•con•o•my, (*n.*), denying ourselves a necessity today in order to buy a luxury tomorrow.

E•con•o•my size, (*n.*), large in soap and small in automobiles.

Ec•sta•sy, (*n.*), "the feeling you feel when you feel you are going to feel a feeling you never felt before."—LARRY WILDE.

Ed•i•tor, (*n.*), "one who separates the wheat from the chaff and prints the chaff."
—ADLAI E. STEVENSON.

Ed•u•ca•tion, (*n.*), "what remains when we have forgotten all that we have been taught."
—GEORGE SAVILE.

Egg, *(n.)*, *1.* a fowl ball. *2.* hen fruit. *3.* A peculiar object, it is not beaten unless it is good. *4.* Like a New Year's resolution, it's so easily broken.

Egg white, *(n.)*, Snow White's brother (get the yolk?).

E go ist, *(n.)*, someone who is always me-deep in conversation.

E go ma ni ac, *(n.)*, *1.* a legend in his own mind. *2.* a person of questionable taste, more interested in himself than in me.

E go tism, *(n.)*, a case of mistaken nonentity.

Eif fel Tow er, *(n.)*, *1.* a French erector set that made good. *2.* the Empire State Building after taxes.

En gage ment, *(n.)*, "a period of urge on the verge of a merge."—UNKNOWN.

Eng lish Chan nel, *(n.)*, the BBC.

En tre pre neur, *(n.)*, like a turtle, not much good until he sticks his neck out a little.

E ras er, *(n.)*, what will take a dozen strokes off any golfer's game.

Eu rope, *(n.)*, the next one at bat.

Ex ec u tive, *(n.)*, a person who never dreamed of earning the salary he can't get along on today.

Ex press way, *(n.)*, a four-lane parking lot.

Fad·dish, (*adj.*), in one era and out the other.

Fair·way, (*n.*), in golf, the well-kept and seldom used area of the course.

Fal·len arch·es, (*n. pl.*), "an affliction of Samson, trolls, and bankrupt McDonald's." —H.G.H.

False friend, (*n.*), someone who is always around when he needs you.

False teeth, (*n. pl.*), like the stars, they come out at night.

Farm, (*n.*), quackers and milk.

Fash·ion, (*n.*), "a form of ugliness so intolerable that we have to alter it every six months."—OSCAR WILDE.

Fa·ther's Day, (*n.*), identical to Mother's Day, only you don't spend as much for the present.

Fil·ing sys·tem, (*n.*), misplacing things in order.

Fine, (*n.*), a tax for doing wrong, as distinguished from a tax, which is a fine for doing all right.

Fire·man, (*n.*), *1.* one always in search of a hot time. *2.* someone willing to make an ash of himself.

Fire·proof, (*adj.*), the boss's relatives.

First love, (*n.*), a comedy of eros.

Fish·ing, (*n.*) "a delusion entirely surrounded by liars in old clothes."—DON MARQUIS.

Fjord, (*n.*), a make of Norwegian automobile.

Flash·light, (*n.*), a case in which to carry dead batteries.

Flood, (*n.*), a river too big for its bridges.

For·eign aid, (*n.*), when the poor people of a rich nation send their money to the rich people of a poor nation.

For·ger, (*n.*), someone who is always ready to write a wrong.

For·tune hunt·er, (*n.*), a widow-shopper.

Fo·rum, (*n.*), two-um plus two-um.

Fowl lan·guage, (*n.*), cheep talk.

Free speech, (*n.*), "calling collect."—H.G.H.

French toast, (*n.*), vive la France.

Friend, (*n.*), *1.* one who visits even if you don't have air conditioning. *2.* one who says nasty things to your face instead of behind your back.

Frog, (*n.*), the only animal with more lives than a cat: it croaks every night.

Gal·lows, *(n.)*, where no noose is good noose.

Gam·bling, *(n.)*, "the art of betting one's hard earned money in hopes of winning it back."
—PAULA STINNETT.

Gar·den, *(n.)*, a plot where most bulbs think they're buried instead of planted.

Gar·den·er, *(n.)*, one who knows that anything that grows like a weed is.

Gar·gling, *(n.)*, the method to discover if your neck leaks.

Ge·ne·al·o·gy, *(n.)*, trying to make a better name for yourself.

Gen·tle·man, *(n.)*, a man who holds the door open for his wife while she carries in the groceries.

Germ, *(n.)*, a microscopic organism that can bring a grown man to his sneeze.

Gift cra·vat, *(n.)*, the tie that blinds.

Gi·raffe, *(n.)*, the highest form of animal life.

Globe·trot·ter, *(n.)*, a traveler with a roamin' nose.

Glut•ton, (*n.*), one who eats too long, as distinguished from a dieter, who longs to eat.

God, (*n.*), believed to be Jewish, having worked a six-day week.

Gol•den wed•ding an•ni•ver•sa•ry, (*n.*), the day when a couple celebrates that 50 years of married life are over.

Golf, (*n.*), a lot like taxes: you drive hard to get to the green and then wind up in the hole.

Go•ril•la, (*n.*), one animal you wouldn't want to monkey around with.

Gos•sip, (*n.*), *1.* a person with a keen sense of rumor. *2.* "that which no one claims to like—but everybody enjoys."—JOSEPH CONRAD. *3.* putting two and two together, and making five.

Gov•ern•ment, (*n.*), *1.* a business where the customer is always wronged. *2.* "The American government is a rule of the people, by the people, for the boss."—AUSTIN O'MALLEY.

Gov•ern•ment spend•ing (*n.*), an explanation of why laws are called bills.

Grand•moth•er, (*n.*), an old lady who keeps your mother from spanking you.

Green, (*adj.*), the color of spring, wealth, fungus and envy.

Hail·ing tax·is, (v.), the only thing worse than raining cats and dogs.

Hair·styl·ing, (v.), shear pleasure.

Half-moon, (n.), "a shy streaker." —H.G.H.

Hang·o·ver, (n.), 1. bottle fatigue. 2. the wrath of grapes. 3. midriff bulge. 4. the moaning after the night before.

Hap·pi·ness, (n.), 1. "a perfume you cannot pour on others without getting a few drops on yourself."—RALPH WALDO EMERSON. 2. "That's nothing more than good health and a poor memory."—ALBERT SCHWEITZER.

Hatch·et, (n.), what a hen does with an egg.

Head·ache, (n.), a pain that's all in your mind.

Heat of pas·sion, (n.), "when you make a fuel of yourself."—H.G.H.

Hel·i·cop·ter, (n.), an eggbeater with ambition.

Hic·cup, (n.), coughing backward.

High cho·les·ter·ol, (n.), a Slobovian religious holiday.

Hijklmno, the formula for water.

Hob·by, (*n.*), something you do to have fun whether you enjoy it or not.

Hole, (*n.*), "nothing at all, but you can break your neck in it."—AUSTIN O'MALLEY.

Hol·ly·wood, (*n.*), "where it isn't who you know, but who you yes."—DAN DURYEA.

Home, (*n.*), a place that, no matter where you are sitting, you're looking at something you should be doing.

Ho·mer, (*n.*), Babe Ruth's Greek agent.

Hoot·en·an·ny, (*n.*), the result of crossing a goat with an owl.

Hor·ror mov·ie, (*n.*), a scream test.

Hors d'oeu·vres, (*n. pl.*), "a ham sandwich cut into forty pieces."—JACK BENNY.

Hu·la, (*n.*), *1.* First you plant a crop of grass on one hip, then plant a crop on the other, and then you rotate the crops. *2.* a shake in the grass.

Hu·man, (*n.*), one who will guffaw at the family album, then look in a mirror and never crack a smile.

Hum·bug, (*n.*), an insect that would sing if it just knew the words.

Hu·mil·i·ty, (*n.*), modesty displayed when people tell you how great you know you are.

Hus·band, (*n.*), a handyman with sex privileges.

Ice sculp·tor, *(n.)*, an artist who finds his success in the deep frieze.

I·deal, *(adj.)*, what you say when it's your turn to distribute the cards.

Im·per·fect past, *(n.)*, what may make future tense.

Im·pos·si·ble, *(adj.)*, "a word only to be found in the dictionary of fools." —NAPOLEON BONAPARTE.

Im·po·tence, *(n.)*, out of ardor.

Im·preg·na·ble, *(adj.)*, incapable of becoming pregnant. —SYN. see *impenetrable; inconceivable; inscrutable; insurmountable; unbearable.*

In·come tax, *(n.)*, what has made more people liars than golf.

In·con·gru·ous, *(adj.)*, where the laws are made.

In·cor·rect·ly, *(adv.)*, the only word always pronounced incorrectly.

In·creas·es, *(n. pl.)*, needing pressing.

In·di·an·ap·o·lis 500, *(n.)*, vrroom at the top.

In·dis·tinct, *(adj.)*, where you pile the dirty dishes.

In·dus·tri·al·ist, (*n.*), one known by the companies he keeps.

In·dus·tri·ous, (*adj.*), getting to work five minutes before the boss.

In·fant prod·i·gy, (*n.*), a baby with highly imaginative parents.

In·fla·tion, (*n.*), what makes it possible for you to live in a more expensive neighborhood without even moving.

In·hi·bi·tion, (*n.*), being tied up in nots.

Ink·ling, (*n.*), a baby fountain pen.

In·stant, (*n.*), the interval between the time the light turns green and the jerk behind you honks his horn.

In·su·late, (*v.*), what teenagers get.

In·sur·ance, (*n.*), "what you pay now so when you're dead you'll have nothing to worry about." —JOSEPH ROSENBLOOM.

In·tel·lec·tu·al, (*n.*), a man who hears the name Monroe and thinks of the doctrine.

In·ves·tor, (*n.*), one who doesn't believe in Santa Claus but is convinced he can beat Wall Street.

I.R.S., (*n.*), "Infernal Revenue Squeeze."—H.G.H.

Is·land, (*n.*), where the bottom of the sea sticks up through the water.

Jeep, (*n.*), man's attempt to create a mechanical mule.

Jew·el·er, (*n.*), a profession with many facets.

Joan of Arc, (*n.*), Noah's wife.

Job, (*n.*), the ideal gift for the man who has nothing.

John Deere let·ter, (*n.*), the result of your gal running off with your tractor.

Jo·nah, (*n.*), "the first interior decorator"—H.G.H.

Jour·nal·ism school, (*n.*), the chamber of commas.

Joy of moth·er·hood, (*n.*), what a woman experiences when all her children are finally in bed.

Judge, (*n.*), a man of many convictions.

Junk, (*n.*), something you keep 20 years and then throw away two weeks before you need it.

Ju·ror, (*n.*), a person who can't make up a good excuse.

Ju·ven·ile de·lin·quen·cy, (*n.*), a contemporary term for what adults did when they were kids.

Kan•ga•roo, (*n.*), nature's original effort to evolve a cheerleader.

Ken•nel, (*n.*), a barking lot.

Ketch•up, (*n.*), what slow runners stride to do.

Kha•ki, (*n.*), what starts a Boston limousine.

Kids, (*n. pl.*), those children who can quietly take no for an answer without letting it disturb their plans.

Kin•der•gar•ten teach•er, (*n.*), a person who knows how to make the little things count.

King, (*n.*), "a highly paid model for a postage stamp."—UNKNOWN.

King Mi•das, (*n.*), a monarch with a gilt complex.

King•pin, (*n.*), what holds up a prince's diaper.

Kiss, (*n.*), an application for a better position.

Kiss•ing, (*v.*), may be the language of love, but money still does all the talking.

Kitch•en•ette, (*n.*), "where the wifette thaws things."—BABE WEBSTER.

K9, (*n.*), "R2D2's mutt."—H.G.H.

Lac·quer, (*n.*), with liquor, the two finishes for an automobile.

La·dy, (*n.*), one who whispers sweet nothing-doings in your ear.

La·dy Go·di·va, (*n.*), An inveterate gambler, she put everything she had on a horse.

Lan·ded gen·try, (*n.*), men who are either married or engaged.

Laugh, (*n.*), "a smile that burst."—JOHN DONOVAN.

Lead·er, (*n.*), "a man who has the ability to make other people do what they don't want to do, and like it."—HARRY S. TRUMAN.

Leap year, (*n.*), "when February has a day that's even rarer than a day in June."—ANON.

Lec·ture, (*n.*), an occasion that makes you feel numb at one end and dumb at the other.

Left·o·vers, (*n. pl.*), *1.* mull-again stew. *2.* "foiled again."—H.G.H.

Leg·end, (*n.*), "a lie that has attained the dignity of age."—ANON.

Leth·ar·gy, (*n.*), when your get up and go got up and went.

Li·brar·i·an, (*n.*), like a glass blower, one who can't whistle while he works.

Life·guard, (*n.*), *1.* tan man. *2.* "roast beef." —H.G.H.

Life in·sur·ance, (*n.*), a policy that keeps you poor all your life so you can die rich.

Lips, (*n. pl.*), the fleshy folds that stop your mouth from fraying around the edges.

Lip·stick, (*n.*), what you wear when you want to keep your mouth shut.

Lit·ter, (*n.*), our grossest national product.

Liv·ing wage, (*n.*), a little more than you're making now.

Lla·ma, (*n.*), an animall that resemblles a camell.

Loaf, (*v.*), an attempt to make both weekends meet.

Love, (*n.*). blind, as distinguished from marriage, which is an eye opener.

Love knots, (*n. pl.*), those that are best tied with a single beau.

Love tri·an·gle, (*n.*), a predicament that quickly shapes into a wrecktangle.

Lum·bar re·gion, (*n.*), the place your back feels stiff as a board.

Mad·ame, *(n. (French))*, a married woman; the difference between a madame and a mademoiselle is a monsieur.

Mad mon·ey, *(n.)*, "a psychiatrist's fee."
—LARRY WILDE.

Maid·en aunt, *(n.)*, a woman who never hollered "uncle."

Man, *(n.)*, a creature who buys football tickets three months in advance and waits until Christmas Eve to do his gift shopping.

Man·goes, *(n. pl.)*, wherever woman goes.

Mar·a·thon, *(n.)*, fleet feet feat.

Mar·riage, *(n.)*, *1.* that which begins when you sink into his arms and ends with your arms in the sink. *2.* learning about the opposite sex the hard way.

Mar·rieds, *(n. pl.)*, those who complain when the sound goes off at a drive-in movie.

Mar·ry, *(v.)*, to join as husband and wife. Future tense: divorce.

Mas·seuse, *(n.)*, a gal who works her fingers to the bone.

Ma•ter•nal love, (*n.*), smotherly love.

Ma•ter•ni•ty clothes, (*n. pl.*), ladies' ready-to-bear.

May-De•cem•ber wed•ding, (*n.*), delusions of glandeur.

Means, (*n. pl.*), limits we are all determined not to live beyond even if we must borrow to do so.

Med•i•cal pro•fes•sion, (*n.*), an association dedicated to preventing people from dying natural deaths.

Mem•o•ry, (*n.*), what you forget with.

Me•ow, (*n.*), the pedantry of a bilingual dog.

Mid•dle age, (*n.*), *1.* the conflict between Mother Nature and Father Time. *2.* when you start eating what is good for you instead of what you like.

Min•er, (*n.*), one who really digs what he's doing.

Mi•ni•skirt, (*n.*), There are three styles: A. two inches above the knee, B. five inches above the knee, C. "Good morning, your honor."

Min•ute, (*n.*), the difference between kissing your brother and your lover.

Min•ute•man, (*n.*), a guy who makes it to the refrigerator and back for a snack during the commercial.

Mir•ror, (*n.*), a device most dieters use to watch what they eat.

Mist, (*n.*), rain that isn't trying very hard.

Mis•take, (*n.*), something a virgin and a parachutist can make only once.

Mis•tress, (*n.*), *1.* something between a mister and a mattress. *2.* what some men take just to break the monogamy.

Mod•el hus•band, (*n.*), any other woman's.

Mo•dern age, (*n.*), "When girls wear less on the street than their grandmothers did in bed."
—UNKNOWN.

Mon•day, (*n.*), a hard way to spend one-seventh of your life.

Mon•ey, (*n.*), "the poor people's credit card."
—MARSHALL McLUHAN.

Mon•u•men•tal li•ar, (*n.*), a writer of epitaphs.

Moon•light•ing, (*n.*), how a vampire makes a living.

Moose, (*n.*), an animal with antlers on one end and a living room wall on the other.

Mor•al•ist, (*n.*), one who insists on his conscience being your guide.

Moth•er-in-law sand•wich, (*n.*), cold shoulder and tongue.

Moth•er Na•ture, (*n.*), "Providential. She gives us twelve years to develop love for our children before turning them into teenagers."—ANON.

Moth•er's Day, (*n.*), nine months after Father's Day.

Moun•tain climb•er, (*n.*), a person who wants to take just one more peak.

Mov•ie, (*n.*), where people with bad coughs go instead of to a doctor.

Mur•der•er, (*n.*), one presumed innocent until proven insane.

Mu•si•cians, (*n. pl.*), the ones at a dance who don't.

Mys•ter•y of life, (*n.*), "how the idiot who married your daughter can be the father of the smartest grandchildren in the world."—ANON.

Nag, (*n.*), a horse so slow, the jockey keeps a diary of the trip.

Na•ive, (*adj.*), thinking someone is interested when they ask how you are.

Neigh•bor, (*n.*), a person who can arrive at your house in a minute, and take hours to go back home.

Nep•o•tism, (*n.*), putting on heirs.

Nerv•ous, (*adj.*), feeling in a hurry all over and not getting started anywhere.

Neu•ro•tic, (*n.*), "A neurotic is the man who builds a castle in the air. A psychotic is the man who lives in it. And a psychiatrist is the man who collects the rent."—UNKNOWN.

New im•proved, (*adj.*), a contradiction in terms.

New York Cit•y, (*n.*), the city of brotherly shove.

Nick•el, (*n.*), "ain't worth a dime anymore." —YOGI BERRA.

Night•gown, (*n.*), nap sack.

No•bod•y, (*n.*), "that which best describes a ghost."—H.G.H.

Noise pol·lu·tion, (*n.*), the main cause of eari-tation.

No·man, (*n.*), an island.

Non·cha·lance, (*n.*), "the quality of looking like an owl when you've acted like an ass."—ANON.

Non-prof·it, (*adj.*), a characteristic of a large number of organizations, many of which did not mean to be.

Nose, (*n.*), the one feature we tend to overlook.

Nos·tal·gia, (*n.*), *1.* "the realization that things weren't as unbearable as they seemed at the time."—HEMAN FAY, JR. *2.* "longing for the place you wouldn't move back to."—JAMES SANAKER.

Nu·cle·ar budg·et, (*n.*), pay as you glow.

Nu·cle·ar phys·i·cist, (*n.*), one whose wife doesn't understand him.

Nu·cle·ar war, (*n.*), "won't be a question of what's right, but rather what's left."
—ALBERT SAVAGE.

Nude, (*adj.*), barefoot all over.

Nud·ist, (*n.*), one who strips to the waist—from both ends.

Nym·pho·ma·ni·ac, (*n.*), a wife who makes love to hubby just after having her hair done.

O·boe, *(n.)*, an ill wind that nobody blows good.

Oc·to·pus, *(n.)*, an eight-legged cat.

Oc·u·list, *(n.)*, a physician with an eye for business.

Off-day, *(n.)*, the day after a day off.

Old age, *(n.)*, *1.* when you know all the answers and nobody asks you the questions. *2.* when everything you have seems to wear out, spread out, or fall out. *3.* when all the names in your little black book end in M.D. *4.* when you get winded playing chess. *5.* when you are 20 around the neck, 50 around the waist, and 123 around the golf course.

Old·est pro·fes·sion, *(n.)*, fruit picking.

One good turn, *(n.)*, what usually gets you all the blanket.

O·pen mind, *(n.)*, often just a hole in the head.

Op·er·a, *(n.)*, where some guy gets stabbed, and instead of dying, he sings.

Op·er·a·tion, *(n.)*, a surgery that takes minutes to perform and years to describe.

Op•por•tun•ist, *(n.)*, *1.* anyone who goes ahead and does what you always intended to do. *2.* one who, finding himself in hot water, decides to take a bath.

Op•ti•cian, *(n.)*, a profession with a lot of contacts.

Op•ti•mism, *(n.)*, waiting for your ship to come in when you haven't sent one out.

Op•ti•mist, *(n.)*, *1.* one who packs a frying pan on a fishing trip. *2.* a bachelor contemplating marriage, as distinguished from a pessimist, who is a married person contemplating marriage. *3.* "sees an opportunity in every calamity; a pessimist sees a calamity in every opportunity."
—WINSTON CHURCHILL.

O•rig•i•nal•i•ty, *(n.)*, "the art of remembering what you hear and forgetting where you heard it."—TOMMY DOUGLAS.

Or•tho•don•tist, *(n.)*, a dentist who'll put the bite on you.

Ouch, *(interj.)*, the sound of two porcupines kissing.

Out•of•bounds, *(adj.)*, a retired kangaroo.

O•ver•weight, *(adj.)*, just desserts.

Pan•ty hose, (*n.*), long janes.

Par•a•dox, (*n.*), M.D.[2]

Par•a•lyze, (*v.*), double double-cross.

Par•ents, (*n. pl.*), a peculiar group who first try to get their children to walk and talk, and then try to get them to sit down and shut up.

Park•ing at•tend•ant, (*n.*), a bang-up job.

Part•ly cloud•y, (*adj.*), a misleading weather term, usually measured in inches.

Pass•port pho•to, (*n.*), the way to see yourself as others see you.

Pas•teur•ize, (*v.*), where your life goes as you're dying.

Pat•ent med•i•cine, (*n.*), not what it's quacked up to be.

Pa•tience, (*n.*), something you admire in the driver behind you but not in the one you're behind.

Pa•tient, (*n.*), *1.* "What I call a good patient is one who, having found a good physician, sticks to him till he dies."—OLIVER WENDELL HOLMES. *2.* "symptoms with relatives attached."—ANON.

Pa•tri•ot, (*n.*), one who is sorry that he has only one income to give to his country.

Pa•tri•ot•ism, (*n.*), "your conviction that this country is superior to all other countries because you were born in it."—GEORGE BERNARD SHAW.

Peace move•ment, (*n.*), a cause that often has trouble sticking to its guns.

Ped•ant•ry, (*n.*), "stupidity that read a book." —UNKNOWN.

Pe•des•tri•an, (*n.*), a fella who has two cars, a wife, and a kid in high school.

Pen•i•cil•lin, (*n.*), the perfect gift for the person who has everything.

Per•fec•tion•ist, (*n.*), a person who takes infinite pains—and usually gives them to everyone around him.

Per•fume, (*n.*), *1.* a scent that leaves you smell-bound. *2.* a substance you pay through the nose for.

Per•ma•nent wave, (*n.*), a lady admiral.

Pes•si•mist, (*n.*), *1.* one who finds bad news in a fortune cookie. *2.* "an optimist on his way home from the race track."—RED SMITH.

Phi•lan•der•er, (*n.*), a man who considers himself too good to be true.

Pho•tog•ra•phy, (*n.*), like love, you never know how it will develop.

Pink car•na•tion, (*n.*), what America would be if all autos were pale red.

Pla•ton•ic friend•ship, (*n.*), "what develops when two people grow tired of making love." —ANON.

Pleas•ure trip, (*n.*), *1.* separate vacations. *2.* driving your mother-in-law to the airport.

Plump, (*adj.*), having a shape like a figure ate.

Poise, (*n.*), the ability to keep right on talking while the other guy picks up the check.

Po•lit•i•cal cam•paign, (*n.*), a matter of mud, threat and smears.

Po•li•ti•cian, (*n.*), someone who can give you his complete attention without hearing a word you say.

Pol•i•tics, (*n.*), the most promising of all careers.

Po•lyg•a•my, (*n.*), proof there can be too much of a good thing.

Poo•dle, (*n.*), what you step in after it rains cats and dogs.

Poor rel•a•tive, (*n.*), one who is touch and go.

Pop mu•sic, (*n.*), what Dad sings in the shower.

Pre•his•tor•ic times, (*n. pl.*), the most widely read newspaper in the Stone Age.

Prim•i•tive art, (*n.*), aboriginals.

Pris•on•er, (*n.*), someone who doesn't mind being interrupted in mid-sentence.

Prog•nos•ti•ca•tion, (*n.*), the ability to foretell, and then explain why it did not happen.

Pro•jec•tion•ist, (*n.*), one who works in the reel world.

Proof•read•er, (*n.*), one who profits by other people's mistakes.

Prude, (*n.*), "one who is troubled by improper thoughts, as distinguished from the rest of us, who rather enjoy them."—BABE WEBSTER.

Psy•chi•a•trist, (*n.*), the person you see when you're going crazy, and he helps you.

Psy•chot•ic, (*n.*), one who thinks that two and two is five, as distinguished from a neurotic who knows two and two is four—but hates it.

Pto•maine, (*n.*), a pterrible ptoxin that causes ptremendous ptrouble in one's ptummy.

Pub•lic•i•ty, (*n.*), notice you get when you're successful and don't need it.

Pump•er•nick•el, (*n.*), due to inflation, see *pumperdime.*

Quack, (*n.*), a veterinarian specializing in sick ducks.

Quad·rup·lets, (*n. pl.*), four crying out loud.

Quar·an·tine, (*n.*), for the person who has everything.

Quar·ter, (*n.*), a dollar with all the taxes taken out.

Quar·tet, (*n.*), four people who think the other three sing off-key.

Quartz, (*n.*), "two pintz."—H.G.H.

Quay, (*n.*), a device that opens a river bank.

Queen bee, (*n.*), the power behind the drone.

Queens, (*n. pl.*), the sport of kings.

Quest, (*n.*), "Love is the quest, marriage the conquest, divorce the inquest."—ANON.

Ques·tion, (*n.*), a whys remark.

Ques·tion·a·ble, (*adj.*), the answer to the question, "Is there a word containing all the vowels?"

Quip, (*n.*), a mini ha-ha.

Rab•bit, (*n.*), the gift that keeps on giving.

Race prob•lem, (*n.*), picking the winner.

Rack•et•eer, (*n.*), a dishonest tennis player.

Ra•di•o an•nounc•er, (*n.*), one who tries to sneak in the commercial before you can change stations.

Raise, (*n.*), an increase of salary just prior to sinking more into debt.

Rai•sin, (*n.*), a worried grape.

Rare vol•ume, (*n.*), a borrowed book that is returned.

Rav•ing beau•ty, (*n.*), "a beauty contest run-ner-up."—H.G.H.

Re•ac•tion•ar•y, (*n.*), "a somnambulist walk-ing backwards."—FRANKLIN D. ROOSEVELT.

Read•ing, (*n.*), "thinking with someone else's head instead of one's own." —ARTHUR SCHOPENHAUER.

Re•al•is•tic toys, (*n. pl.*), ones that don't work half the time.

Re·ap·pear·ance, (*n.*), an anatomical part, as in, "He kissed her upon her reappearance."

Re·cep·tion, (*n.*), a party without chairs.

Re·cess, (*n.*), teacher's coffee break.

Re·ces·sion, (*n.*), "It's a recession when your neighbor loses his job; it's a depression when you lose yours."—HARRY S. TRUMAN

Reck·less drunk, (*n.*), seldom a wreckless driver.

Red light, (*n.*), where the tortoise and hare meet once again.

Re·duce, (*v.*), a word to the wide.

Re·frig·er·a·tor, (*n.*), "a place where you store leftovers until they're old enough to throw out."
—AL BOLISKA.

Re·gat·ta, (*n.*), a sails meeting.

Re·gret, (*n.*), insight that comes a day too late.

Rein·deer, (*n.*), "sled propulsion. Note: the most famous were Santa's 8-team introduced in 1822 in Dr. Clement Clarke Moore's poem, 'A Visit from St. Nicholas,' and were named, if memory serves: Dachshund, Dandruff, Panzer and Nixon; Combat, Stupid, Dunghill and Blitzkrieg."
—H.G.H.

Rel·a·tives, (*n. pl.*), "like radishes. Just when you think you've heard the last of them, there they is again."—THE KINGFISH.

Re·li·gion, (*n.*), what too many of us spend too much time arguing about without having any.

Ren·e·gade, (*n.*), in politics, one who abandons your party for the opposition, as distinguished from a convert, who leaves his party to join yours.

Ren·o·vat·ed, (*adj.*), divorced in Nevada.

Rep·ar·tee, (*n.*), saying what you think after becoming a departee.

Re·peal, (*v.*), a strip teaser's encore.

Re·sort, (*n.*), a place where you vacation so the natives can afford to live there the rest of the year.

Res·ti·tu·tion, (*n.*), "a hotel or motel."—H.G.H.

Rest·room, (*n.*), "There's no difference between the restroom and the grave—when ya gotta go, ya gotta go."—ANON.

Ret·i·cence, (*n.*), knowing what you're talking about but keeping your mouth shut.

Re·tire·ment, (*n.*), an occasion when time is no longer important and your employer presents you with a watch.

Rheu·ma·tism, (*n.*), nature's first weather forecaster.

Rich man, (*n.*), *1.* one who's not afraid to ask the clerk to show him something cheaper. *2.* a man so wealthy he's unaware his children are in college.

Right guard, (*n.*), the best-smelling athlete on the team.

Rip van Win•kle, (*n.*), "Some guy who was able to sleep for twenty years because his neighbors didn't have televisions."—UNKNOWN.

Rob•in, (*n.*), a hood that done good.

Rock•et, (*n.*), what you do to a cradle.

Ro•de•o per•form•er, (*n.*), like a politician, someone who makes a living throwing the bull.

Roost•er, (*n.*), an alarm cluck.

Rose, (*n.*), *1.* rose. *2.* rose.

Roth•schild, (*n.*), "magnum cum laude."—H.G.H.

Rub•ber check, (*n.*), one that bounces back, and may cause you to serve a long stretch.

Run•a•way best•sell•er, (*n.*), "Huck Finn." —H.G.H.

Rus•sia, (*n.*), "a riddle wrapped in a mystery inside an enigma."—WINSTON CHURCHILL.

Rus•sian danc•ing, (*n.*), running while sitting down.

Sa•ble, (*n.*), the skin girls love to touch.

Sad•ist, (*n.*), "someone who is kind to masochists."
—VINCENT McHUGH.

Saint, (*n.*), your wife's first husband.

Sales re•sist•ance, (*n.*), the triumph of mind over patter.

Salt, (*n.*), a seasoning that makes potatoes taste lousy when you boil them and don't put any in.

School, (*n.*), an institution where children go to catch cold from other children so they can stay home.

School lunch, (*n.*), a contradiction in terms.

Sci•ence, (*n.*), "an orderly arrangement of what at the moment seem to be facts.—ANON.

Scis•sors, (*n. pl.*), the only thing that will cut your utility bills.

Sculp•tor, (*n.*), an old chiseler who takes things for granite.

Sé•ance, (*n.*), doing what comes supernaturally.

Sec•ond•a•ry, (*adj.*), where to go if the first one is out of milk.

Se•cret of youth, (*n.*), lie about your age.

Self-re•straint, (*n.*), the ability to resist a temptation in the hope that a better one will come along.

Sense of hu•mor, (*n.*), the ability to laugh at something which would make you mad if it happened to you.

Sev•en ag•es of wom•an, (*n. pl.*), "baby, child, girl, young woman, young woman, young woman, and poised social leader."—ANON.

Sex, (*n.*), *1.* the only time one and one make three. *2.* the only three-letter four-letter word in our language.

Shake hands, (*v.*), what a dog does on three legs, a man standing up, and a woman sitting down.

Shell shock, (*n.*), the result of eating peanuts in bed.

Shock treat•ment, (*n.*), when doctors bill in advance.

Shoe fet•ish•ist, (*n.*), one excited by Freudian slippers.

Shore leave, (*n.*), wolves in ship's clothing.

Short•cut, (*n.*), the longest distance between two points.

Shot•gun wed•ding, (*n.*), a matter of wife or death.

Shrunk, (*v.*), a retired psychiatrist.

Si•lence, (*n.*), reputedly golden, which may explain its scarcity.

Sin, (*n.*), "Sin and dandelions are very much alike. To get rid of them is a lifetime fight, and you never quite win it."—WILLIAM ALLEN WHITE.

Sins of o•mis•sion, (*n. pl.*), the sins we wish we had committed, and didn't.

Sit•u•ate, (*v.*), what happens when you arrive early for your doctor's appointment.

Skel•e•ton, (*n.*), bones with the person scraped off.

Skirt, (*n.*), what girls wear shorter to make guys look longer.

Sledge ham•mer, (*n.*), the best method for beating a slot machine.

Slip cov•er, (*n.*), a maternity outfit.

Small town, (*n.*), a town so small that: *1.* everybody knows what everybody else is doing, but they read the local newspaper anyhow to see who got caught at it; *2.* the barbershop quartet is a trio.

Smoke a•larm, (*n.*), "a device to remind a bachelor that the meat loaf is done."—H.G.H.

Snack, (*n.*), the pause that refleshes.

So•cial•ist, (*n.*), one who has nothing and wants you to divide with him.

So•ci•e•ty, (*n.*), "consists of two classes: the lower class cultivates the dignity of labor, the upper class the labor of dignity."—UNKNOWN.

Sound ad•vice, (*n.*), usually 90% sound and 10% advice.

Span•ish weath•er fore•cast, (*n.*), "Chili today, hot tamale."

Speed lim•it, (*n.*), to a teen-ager, defined as what his car will do.

Spin•ster, (*n.*), a bachelor's wife.

Splits, (*n. pl.*), what Moses did at the Red Sea.

Square dance, (*n.*), a prom for folks over 30.

State of mat•ri•mo•ny, (*n.*), "the only state populated half slave and half free."—ANON.

Steam, (*n.*), water gone crazy with the heat.

Steel wool, (*n.*), what wolves do.

Sto•ic, (*adj.*), de boid what brings de babies.

Stole, (*n.*), a burglar's present to his wife.

Stork, (*n.*), "a bird that is frequently called to account for misdemeanors which should really be blamed on a lark."—UNKNOWN.

Strap·less gown, (*n.*), "a compromise between the law of decency and the law of gravity." —UNKNOWN.

Strip pok·er, (*n.*), panty ante.

Strip tease, (*n.*), grin and bare it.

Suc·cess, (*n.*), the ability to get along with some people—and ahead of others.

Sug·ar dad·dy, (*n.*), "a gent who calls his sweetie sugar and later pays her a lump sum."—ANON.

Sug·ges·tion, (*n.*), a hintimation.

Sum·mer camp, (*n.*), where kids go for their parents' vacations.

Sun and air, (*n.*), who inherits the wind.

Sure·foot·ed mule, (*n.*), one that kicks you twice in the same place.

Swim·ming pool, (*n.*), a can of people packed in water.

Sym·pa·thy, (*n.*), what one person offers another in exchange for details.

Syn·tax, (*n.*), the price of vice.

Ta·co Bell, (*n.*), the Mexican phone company.

Tact, (*n.*), *1.* "the art of making a point without making an enemy."—HOWARD NEWTON. *2.* "consists in knowing how far to go too far."—JEAN COCTEAU. *3.* "the ability to give a person a shot in the arm without letting him feel the needle." —ORLANDO ALOYSIUS BATTISTA.

Take-home pay, (*n.*), so called because it's the only place you can afford to go with it.

Tan·gent, (*n.*), the guy just back from the beach.

Tan·ning sa lon, (*n.*), where no stern is left untoned.

Tap danc·er, (*n.*), a hoofer with music in her sole.

Tape·worm, (*n.*), another mouth to feed.

Tat·too·er, (*n.*), an artist who needles his customers to get the point.

Tax col·lec·tor, (*n.*), "There is one difference between a tax collector and a taxidermist—the taxidermist leaves the hide."—VAR. ATTRIB.

Tax cut, (*n.*), the kindest cut of all.

Tax•pay•er, (*n.*), someone who has the entire government on his payroll.

T. Boone Pick•ens, Jr., doll, (*n.*), Wind it up and it buys you out.

Teach•er, (*n.*), one who trains the mind, as distinguished from a conductor, who minds the train.

Tea•pot, (*n.*), what begins with T, ends with T, and has T in it.

Tee shot, (*n.*), for many duffers, an unplayable lie.

Teen age, (*adj.*), "when your children finally get old enough that you can stand them and then they can't stand you."—ANON.

Teen-ag•er, (*n.*), a kid who thinks that curbing his emotions means parking by the roadside.

Tel•e•phone, (*n.*), what never asks questions but is often answered.

Tel•e•phone op•er•a•tor, (*n.*), a worker who suffers constant ringing in the ears.

Tel•e•vi•sion, (*n.*), *1.* a boob-tube. *2.* a vidiot's delight. *3.* "chewing gum for the eyes."
—JOHN MASON BROWN.

Tem•per•a•men•tal, (*adj.*), 90% temper, 10% mental.

Tem•per tan•trum, (*n.*), call of the riled.

Temp•ta•tion, (*n.*), an irresistible force at work on a movable body.

Tex•as, (*n.*), miles and miles of miles and miles.

TGIF, what Robinson Crusoe said after discovering footprints in the sand.

The•o•ry, (*n.*), a hunch with higher education.

The•sau•rus, (*n.*), "a dinosaur with a highly developed vocabulary."—NICK SIEGLER.

Think, (*v.*), "what you do if you can't thwim."
—MARY WALTER NOESS.

Think tank, (*n.*), "close encounters of the nerd kind."—H.G.H.

Thir•ty-five, (*adj.*), "a very attractive age; London society is full of women who have of their own free choice remained thirty-five for years."
—OSCAR WILDE.

Three-year-old child, (*n.*), "a being who gets almost as much fun out of a fifty-six-dollar set of swings as it does out of finding a small green worm."—BILL VAUGHAN.

Tin an•ni•ver•sa•ry, (*n.*), a 10-year celebration of eating out of cans.

Tips, (*n. pl.*) wages we pay other people's help.

To•mor•row, (*n.*), what is always coming but will never arrive.

Tongue, (*n.*), "A sharp tongue is the only edge tool that grows keener with constant use." —WASHINGTON IRVING.

Tongue twist•er, (*n.*), an expression that gets your tang tongueled.

Tooth•paste, (*n.*), stuff that helps keep your teeth stuck in your head.

Torch sing•er, (*n.*), "a woman who lights a fire that the customers put out with liquor."—ANON.

To•ron•to, (*n.*), "Kimosabe's Canadian companion."—H.G.H.

Tor•ture, (*n.*) "Some tortures are physical and some are mental. But the one that's both is dental."—UNKNOWN.

Tour•ist, (*n.*), a person who travels 2,000 miles to have his picture taken standing beside his car.

Trade re•la•tions, (*n. pl.*), what most people would like to do.

Traf•fic, (*n.*), a mass of cars moving quickly until your car joins them.

Train, (*n.*), what people miss most when they move to the suburbs.

Tram•po•line art•ist, (*n.*), like an elevator operator, a job with lots of ups and downs.

Trav•el, (*n.*), what is believed will broaden the mind, but it usually just lengthens the conversation.

Trav•el a•gent, (*n.*), a leisure time placement engineer.

Tree sur•geon, (*n.*), the only doctor who can fall out of his patient.

Tri•an•gle, (*n.*), a circle with three corners.

Trom•bon•ist, (*n.*), a musician who has learned to let things slide.

Truth, (*n.*), *1.* "like a bird, is ever poised for flight at man's approach."—JEAN BROWN. *2.* "is always strange—stranger than fiction." —GEORGE GORDON BYRON.

Tube, (*n.*), or not tube.

Tu•tor, (*n.*), a trumpet teacher.

Twen•ty-five, (*adj.*), "the proper age for a woman; if she is not proper by that time, she never will be."—UNKNOWN.

Twins, (*n. pl.*), womb mates.

Ty•po•graph•i•cal er•rors, (*n. pl.*), slips that pass in the write.

UCLA, "what happens when the smog lifts."—H.G.H.

UFO, unidentified freezer object.

Um·brel·la, (*n.*), an oddity that is most useful when it's used up.

Un·a·bridged, (*adj.*), "a river that keeps you wading."—H.G.H.

Un·a·ware, (*adj.*), what your mother always told you to wear clean in case of an accident.

Un·can·ny, (*adj.*), the way grandmother prepared meals.

Un·cle Sam, (*n.*), kin we all owe a great deal.

Un·der·arm pro·tec·tion, (*n.*), "a shoulder-holstered pistol."—H.G.H.

Un·der·ground e·con·o·my, (*n.*), land of untold wealth.

Un·der·priv·i·leged, (*adj.*), "The poor became 'needy;' the needy were elevated to 'deprived;' and the deprived were promoted to 'underprivileged.' They still have no money, but they have acquired a vocabulary."—WILLIAM LAMBDIN.

Un·der·rate, (*v.*), seven or less.

Un·faith·ful, (*adj.*), "having nothing to say to your husband because you've already said everything to someone else."—FRANÇOISE SAGAN.

Un·ion rate, (*n.*), wedding fee.

U·nit·ed States, (*n. pl.*), a country covered one-quarter by forests and the rest by mortgages.

U·ni·ver·si·ty, (*n.*), *1.* "a place where pebbles are polished and diamonds are dimmed." —ROBERT INGERSOLL. *2.* a school which has room for 4,000 in its classrooms and 80,000 in its stadium.

Un·known, (*adj.*), *1.* "an effusive though elusive author."—UNKNOWN. *2.* "the second most famous and prolific of all writers." —ANON.

Un·law·ful, (*adj.*), against the law, as distinguished from illegal, which is a sick bird.

USA, "the only country where a housewife hires a woman to do her cleaning so she can do volunteer work at the day nursery where the cleaning woman leaves her child."—BOB PHILLIPS.

Used car, (*n.*), a secondhand automobile in first-crash condition.

US Mint, (*n.*), a company where workers threaten to strike unless they make less money.

U·su·rer, (*n.*), a man who takes too much interest in his business.

Va·ca·tion, *(n.)*, *1.* something you take when you can't take what you're taking. *2.* 2 weeks that are 2 short after which you are 2 tired 2 return 2 work and 2 broke not 2.

Vac·u·um, *(n.)*, the distance between some people's ears.

Val·et park·ing, *(n.)*, skid row.

Vam·pire, *(n.)*, a pain in the neck.

Vam·pir·ism, *(n.)*, love in vein.

Van·ish·ing A·mer·i·can, *(n.)*, one who pays cash.

Vas·ec·to·my, *(n.)*, never having to say you're sorry.

Veg·e·tar·i·an, *(n.)*, a good salad citizen.

Vend·ing ma·chine, *(n.)*, a gambling device.

Ve·ne·re·al dis·ease, *(n.)*, the gift that keeps on giving.

Ve·nus de Mi·lo, *(n.)*, "the goddess of disarmament."—LEONARD LOUIS LEVINSON.

Ver·bose, *(adj.)*, mighty mouth.

Vice pres•i•dent, (*n.*), *1.* "a spare tire on the automobile of government."—JOHN NANCE GARNER. *2.* "a title given in lieu of a salary raise." —H.G.H.

Vir•gin, (*n.*), *1.* a female who hasn't met her maker. *2.* a girl who ran all the way home because she was being chaste.

Vir•tue, (*n.*), just vice at rest.

Vi•rus, (*n.*), a Latin word meaning "Your guess is as good as mine."

Vis•i•tors, (*n. pl.*), those who always give pleasure—if not by their coming, then by their going.

Vis•ta, (*n.*), "an opening in the landscape through which one can see a billboard."—UNKNOWN.

Vol•ca•no, (*n.*), a mountain that has blown its stack and flipped its lid.

Vo•lup•tu•ous wom•an, (*n.*), "one who has curves in places where some girls don't even have places."—HENNY YOUNGMAN.

Vot•er, (*n.*), "There are two types: those who vote for your candidate, and a bunch of ignorant, prejudiced fools."—ANON.

Vot•ing, (*n.*), "a process of standing in line to decide which party will waste your money." —BABE WEBSTER

Waf·fle, (*n.*), a pancake with a non-skid tread.

Walk·ie-talk·ie, (*n.*), the result of crossing a parrot with a centipede.

Walk·ing dis·tance, (*n.*), to teenagers, the space between the telephone and the garage.

Wall·pap·er, (*n.*), a put-up job.

War·den, (*n.*), one who makes his living by the pen.

Wart hog, (*n.*), the result of crossing a pig with a frog.

Wash and wear, (*adj.*), freedom from the press.

Wash·ing·ton, George, (*n.*), "the only President who didn't blame the previous administration for all his troubles."—HUBERT H. HUMPHREY.

Watch dog, (*n.*), the one full of ticks.

Wa·ter·course, (*n.*), how mermaids multiply.

Wed·ding ring, (*n.*), a tourniquet worn on the left hand to stop circulation.

West Point·er, (*n.*), Horace Greeley.

Whal•er, (*n.*), Like a handkerchief, it has stood many a blow and has often been round the horn.

Wheel, (*n.*), "man's greatest invention until he got behind it."—BILL IRELAND.

White-col•lar work•er, (*n.*), one who carries lunch in a briefcase instead of a pail.

Wife, (*n.*), *1.* a mate who complains she has nothing to wear and needs several closets to keep it in. *2.* The difference between a wife and a mistress is night and day.

Wind, (*n.*), *1.* air in a hurry. *2.* sailboat fuel.

Wind chill fac•tor, (*n.*), the meteorological component that, when combined with the heat index, will yield the actual temperature.

Win•ter, (*n.*), the season when we try to keep our house as warm as it was in the summer when we complained about the heat.

Witch•craft, (*n.*), a broom.

Wom•an, (*n.*), *1.* "the female of the human species, and not a different kind of animal." —GEORGE BERNARD SHAW. *2.* one who has no trouble separating the men from the boys.

Work, (*n.*), "the curse of the drinking classes." —OSCAR WILDE.

World, (*n.*), a big ball that revolves on its taxes.

Worm, (*n.*), a snake with no ambition.

Xmas, (*n.*), Buy now, pray later.

X-ray, (*n.*), bellyvision.

X-ray tech·ni·cian, (*n.*), one with inside information.

Xy·lo·phone, (*n.*), what you call a xylo on.

Yale, (*n.*), "a period in a man's life between change of voice and selling insurance."—ANON.

Yank, (*n.*), a dentist of American extraction.

Yard, (*n.*), something that has three feet but can't walk.

Yawn, (*n.*), "a silent shout."—G. K. CHESTERTON.

Yes, (*adv.*), the answer to any question the boss asks.

Ye·ti cock·tail, (*n.*), two and you're abominable.

Young·er gen·er·a·tion, (*n.*), a group alike in many disrespects.

Youth, (*n.*), *1.* one too young to work but old enough to drive a $20,000 car at 90 mph. *2.* as distinguished from childhood and middle age, is that brief period when the sexes talk to each other at parties.

Ze·bra, *(n.),* *1.* a sports-model jackass. *2.* the largest size a woman can buy.

Ze·ro, *(n.),* *1.* the amount of dirt in a hole 3 feet deep, 4 feet wide and 5 feet long. *2.* the number of liberals who have been mugged and are still liberals.

Zinc, *(n.),* where one washes dirty dishes.

Zoo, *(n.),* "a place devised for animals to study the habitats of human beings."—OLIVER HERFORD.

Zoo keep·er, *(n.),* a critter sitter.

Z row, *(n.),* the coldest place in the theater.